KLIMT

by Susanna Partsch

With 32 colour plates and
27 drawings

STUDIO EDITIONS

LONDON

The publishers would like to thank all museums,
archives, galleries and private collectors for their
kind permission to reproduce the drawings and
paintings of Gustav Klimt.

Cover illustrations:
front – Portrait of Adele Bloch-Bauer I, 1907 (section)
back – Buchenwald I, 1902

Originally published 1990 by
International Publishing GmbH, Munich

This English edition published 1990 by
Studio Editions Ltd, Princess House,
50 Eastcastle Street, London W1N 7AP, England

Translated by Charity Scott Stokes

Reprographics by Fotolito Longo AG, Frangart
Typeset by Satz & Repro Grieb, Munich
Printed and bound by Brepols SA, Turnhout, Belgium

ISBN 1 85170 616 X

Klimt's early years

Embracing lovers swathed in fine flowing robes against a gold setting, beautiful and decorative women, lascivious women, female figures shaped like fish or snakes, gold, gold and more gold – that is what springs to mind nowadays when Gustav Klimt's name is mentioned. Little is said about his landscape paintings, his drawings, the early work done on the Vienna Ring. Yet the so-called 'Golden Period' lasted only four years, from 1906 to 1909, and there are many important paintings and drawings from earlier and later dates.

Gustav Klimt was born on 14 July 1862 in Baumgarten, a suburb of Vienna. He was the second of the seven children of the engraver Ernst Klimt (1834–1892) and his wife Anna, née Finster (1836–1915). The family lived in modest circumstances. After the crash of 1873, following the World Exhibition, the Klimts encountered serious financial difficulties. Gustav spent eight years at the Vienna city school. On the advice of his teachers he then applied for admission to the School of Arts and Crafts which had been founded some ten years earlier. He was admitted to the three-year teachers' course. One year later Gustav's brother Ernst was also admitted to the course, and as the brothers both received scholarships the family finances improved. After a short time the brothers were able to supplement their income by assisting their teachers with commissions for work in Arts and Crafts. Another student who was active in this way was Franz Matsch (1861–1942), whose acquaintance Gustav Klimt had made on the occasion of the entrance examination.

At the end of the three-year course the Klimt brothers and Franz Matsch were all given the opportunity to continue their training in the Department of Painting and Decorative Art. They received further relatively generous grants for their studies. Their teacher Ferdinand Laufberger (1829–1881) encouraged them to set up a joint studio, and he procured the first commissions for them.

Their Company of Artists was set up in 1881, two years before the completion of their studies. The three young painters undertook to work more rapidly than would have been possible for one artist on his own, while guaranteeing uniformity of style. Their business flourished, largely because they saw themselves as versatile decorative artists, capable of working in a variety of styles, rather than as individual painters.

One of the first commissions they received, and one which was to occupy them at intervals for a number of years, was the collaborative work on the compendium 'Allegory and Emblem'. It was of great significance for the development of Gustav Klimt's draughtsmanship. In 1882 the Company of Artists received the first of many commissions to work on the interior decoration of a theatre. Their first notable achievement in the capital was the contract for two ceilings in the Villa Hermes in Lainz, just outside Vienna, belonging to the Empress. This turned out so well that the three artists were commissioned to decorate the stairways of Vienna's new Burg Theatre and of the Art History Museum. Gustav Klimt and Franz Matsch also painted two pictures of the interior of the old Burg Theatre before it was demolished. In 1890 these pictures won them the Emperor's Prize, with 400 guilders. During the following year, the work in the Art History Museum was completed.

Half-length sketch of laughing girl,
front view, 1895/96
Black crayon, 44.8 × 31.7 cm

The three artists had established their reputation in Vienna and were accepted as members of the Artists' House.

They could not, however, sustain uniformity of style. By this time Gustav Klimt was moving away from historicism. The first signs of a change of style can be discerned in the 1889 'Allegory of Sculpture', and the new developments can be traced through some of the figures in the stairway of the Art History Museum, becoming more pronounced in the contributions to the third volume of 'Allegory and Emblem'. In the upright rectangular painting 'Love' of 1895 Klimt is clearly engaging with Jugendstil, and in this picture may be found several motifs which were often to recur in his work from this time on: the lovers, still in anticipation of the kiss, are accompanied by the three ages of man and by death. The central part of the picture is bordered by two bands of gold.

The Company of Artists, or what was left of it, was dissolved in 1894. Ernst Klimt had died in 1892. Franz Matsch and Gustav Klimt had grown apart not only as artists but also in their private lives, since Matsch was determined to gain a foothold in Viennese society. His efforts were rewarded, and in 1912 he was elevated to the hereditary aristocracy.

Seated female figure, left arm on
arm-rest (Adele Bloch-Bauer), 1903/04
Pencil, 45 × 31.5 cm

The Vienna Secession

In 1891 Gustav Klimt had become a member of the Vienna Society of
Visual Artists with its headquarters in the Artists' House on the Ring. It
was the only artists' association in the capital, and its established
members had considerable power. Its exhibitions provided the only
opportunity for young artists to become known, but the collection of
work for the exhibitions was made by the association's jury. The old
historicist painters had strong commercial interests which were not
favourable towards new departures or foreign artists. Young members
of the association became increasingly dissatisfied with these conditions and there were several confrontations. In 1897 the Vienna
Secession broke away, with Gustav Klimt as its first president.

The Secessionists had clear ideas which were laid down in their
constitution: they wanted to promote the interests of art only, to keep
their exhibitions free of commercial considerations and to establish
active contacts with foreign artists. Responsibility for organising
exhibitions rested with a small number of individuals.

The architect Josef Maria Olbrich (1867–1908) designed the new

Striding woman, right arm dropping,
left arm extended, 1907
Pencil, 55.9 × 37.1 cm

exhibition building, completed in November 1898. This new building housed major exhibitions during the following years, in which the Viennese public had their first opportunity to see, for instance, arts and crafts from abroad, Japanese art, and French Impressionist painting. There were usually polemics in the press, particularly when Klimt's paintings were on show.

The first occasion for polemics of this sort was provided by Klimt's 'Pallas Athene' in the Secession's second exhibition, of 1898, and notable further occasions were provided by the Faculty pictures and the Beethoven Frieze.

In 1894 Gustav Klimt and Franz Matsch, still working together, had received the joint commission to paint five pictures for the ceiling of the Great Hall of the New University. Four were to represent the four Faculties, and the fifth the 'Triumph of Light over Darkness'. Matsch was responsible for the central picture and for 'Theology', Klimt for 'Philosophy', 'Medicine' and 'Jurisprudence'.

Girl with downcast eyes, 1910/12
Pencil, 55.9 × 37.1 cm

Between 1894 and the date of completion of the pictures, 1907, Klimt's development from historicist painter to Secessionist had taken place. The pictures provide vivid evidence of this development. They were subjected to criticism by the public and by those who had commissioned them, such that Klimt never again undertook an official commission. For years he fought to have them recognised, but in the end he resigned himself to the fact that they would never be displayed in the place for which they were intended, and with the help of private collectors he bought them back again. These three pictures, so important for the development of Klimt's style, were burnt on 8 May 1945 when retreating SS troops set fire to Schloss Immendorf in order to prevent the treasures stored there from falling into Russian hands.

In 1900 'Philosophy' could be viewed for the first time at the Secession's seventh exhibition; 87 professors protested against the picture being mounted on the ceiling of the Great Hall. Opinions of the picture were very different in Paris, where, at the World Exhibition in the autumn of the same year, this picture won Klimt the Gold Medal for a Foreign Artist. In 1901 the presentation of 'Medicine' caused similar reactions in Vienna. In 1903 the Secession showed all three pictures in an exhibition devoted to Klimt's work. Suggestions that the pictures might be hung in the Modern Gallery moved Klimt to buy them back again. In 1907 they were shown once more in their final form, though not in the Secession House, since Klimt had by that time left the Secession.

Klimt experienced a similar public response to his Beethoven Frieze, which was created for one particular exhibition, but which has survived to the present day. Like the Faculty pictures, the frieze represents an important step in Klimt's development.

On 15 April 1902 the Secession's fourteenth exhibition was opened, and it fulfilled a long-held desire, namely the wish to create the 'total work of art'. Architecture, sculpture, painting, crafts – all were subordinated to the central idea, that of the Beethoven sculpture by Max Klinger (1857– 1920) which was nearing completion in 1901. The figure stood in the main hall, accompanied only by frescos, embossed copper plating, sculptures and furniture. The main hall was flanked by two further halls. The one on the right contained frescos based on Schiller's 'Ode to Joy', the final chorus from Beethoven's Ninth Symphony, with jewelled plating beneath the frescos. The hall on the left, which also provided access to the exhibition, was reserved for Gustav Klimt. Here too, beneath the frieze, was jewelled plating. All the decoration was dismantled after the exhibition, and destroyed, except for Klimt's frieze, which was to be shown at the Secession's eighteenth exhibition, devoted to his work. The frieze was privately sold. In 1973 it passed into public ownership, and since 1985 it has been on show once more, after extensive restoration work.

Crouching girl, 1903
Blue pencil, 30.6 × 44.6 cm

Sketch of tall hat and recumbent figure,
1907/08
Lead and red pencil, 55.9 × 37.1 cm

The Beethoven Frieze marks the beginning of Klimt's 'Golden Period'. He drew on Beethoven's Ninth Symphony as interpreted by Richard Wagner (1813–1883), who secured for it a prominent place in musical history. The theme of the frieze, which extended over the two long walls and one end wall of the room, is 'Yearning for Happiness', which, after the defeat of the 'Hostile Forces' with the aid of the 'Strong One in Armour', finds 'Assuagement in Poetry', and then attains the 'Ideal Realm', sole source of 'Pure Joy', 'Pure Happiness', 'Pure Love'. The titles of the separate sections, listed in the exhibition catalogue, were provided by Klimt himself. He was clearly inspired not only by Wagner's interpretation but also by the actual music. His visual realisation of the music transposed notes into pictures and colours, and themes into whole scenes.

The fatalism which prevailed in the three Faculty pictures has given way to the search for salvation. This turning-point in Klimt's oeuvre is marked by the full development of his linear style. Relinquishing

9

Recumbent figure turned half to the left,
1912/13
Pencil, 31. × 51.7 cm

perspective, he reduces his paintings to two dimensions. The art of the line is developed to the fullest extent, giving the figures a sense of incorporeality. The same linear style can be observed in the study drawings Klimt made for the frieze.

The use of a variety of materials shows a tendency towards handicraft work typical of the Secession. The architect Josef Hoffmann (1870–1956) and the painter Koloman Moser (1868–1918) did much to promote arts and crafts. In 1900 they organised an exhibition with works by various English artists and craftsmen who had influenced them. These interests led to the founding of the Vienna Workshops in 1903. Although Klimt was not himself one of the initiators, he and the other Secessionists – artists of the new style – were closely linked with the Workshops.

The Secession had not set out to break new ground in art, but to defend art against commercialisation. Over the years two groups developed. Some of the Secessionists rejected not only traditional historicism, but also Impressionist art; they sought to unite all art forms under the banner of decorative or applied art, and their efforts were rewarded by unexpected acclaim at home and abroad. The naturalists, on the other hand, defended Impressionist art. For them the prime aim was to paint self-sufficient pictures, and today they might be termed 'defenders of the autonomy of the work of art'.

These opposite tendencies enabled the Secessionists to provide a remarkably varied series of exhibitions, but when the efforts of the artists of the new style culminated in the founding of the Vienna Workshops the naturalist group felt excluded, and this resulted in antagonism. In 1904 the Secessionists were prevented from showing their work at the World Exhibition in St Louis by Hoffmann and Klimt's manoeuvres, and when

10

Recumbent figure, 1912/13
Pencil, 36.8 × 55.9 cm

their group also attempted to combine the interests of a commercial gallery with the Secession the naturalists opposed them. Matters came to a head in 1905, and Klimt's group was outvoted by a majority of one. The artists of the new style left the Secession, and the Workshops became the focal point of Jugendstil in Vienna.

During his years with the Secession Klimt had had to face the greatest antagonism to date but he had also begun a second career and had once more achieved notable success. Society women commissioned portraits in the decorative and radiant 'golden style'. Apart from the portraits and the large-scale public pieces, in which life and death were recurrent themes, Klimt was also painting landscapes. The landscape paintings had much to do with a woman who was of paramount importance in his life.

Emilie Flöge

One year before his death, Ernst Klimt had married Helene Flöge (1871–1936). Gustav Klimt was appointed guardian to the daughter of this brief marriage, as a result of which he was a frequent guest in the Flöge household and came to know Helene's younger sister Emilie (1874–1952) very well. By 1897 at the latest they had become close friends, and Klimt's biographers have speculated about the nature and intensity of this friendship, in the absence of concrete facts. Emilie has been seen by some as the self-sacrificing companion of the artist whose sensibilities precluded marriage.

She was, however, an independent woman, and very successful in her own right. In 1904 she and her two sisters founded a fashion salon which was frequented by the wealthy women of Vienna, those same women who commissioned Klimt's portraits. The Flöge Sisters' Fashion House was decorated and furnished by the Vienna Workshops. Twice a year Emilie Flöge travelled to Paris in order to buy designs and materials from such houses as Coco Chanel and Rodier, but Klimt designed garments for her as well. These 'reform clothes' were tailored in the salon for Emilie, and Klimt took photographs of her wearing them in his studio garden, attesting a close professional as well as personal relationship between them.

From 1898 on, Klimt joined the Flöge family for their summer holiday by the Attersee, and it was during these holidays that he began painting landscapes. 54 pictures in all, a quarter of his oeuvre, were painted during these summer months in the Salzkammergut. Many people from Vienna had places of their own in the area, while others rented accommodation for the summer. The Flöge sisters usually left for the country while Klimt was still busy meeting deadlines in Vienna. Sooner or later he would pack up his belongings, especially paints and canvas, and follow them. He sailed and rowed on the Attersee, and later became one of the first Austrians to have his own motor boat. Whether boating or walking, he was usually accompanied by Emilie.

He painted the landscapes that he saw around him on land or water, and all his landscape paintings are of the area round the Attersee even though some of them were completed in Vienna. This explains why Klimt never painted winter landscapes. Summer and early autumn were the seasons for landscape painting, winter and spring belonged with other themes.

Only three landscape drawings have survived, in the few remaining sketchbooks in which Klimt recorded ideas as they came to him. There

Prone figure turned to the right, 1901
Black crayon, 30.5 × 44.8 cm

Pregnant woman with man, 1902
Blue and orange crayon, 44.8 × 30.5 cm

was no need for the figure studies which preceded the large-scale paintings.

Klimt painted out of doors – often, in later years, sitting in his motor boat. In this he resembled the Impressionists, and was unlike the later French painters, who painted indoors from memory, and unlike the artists of the new style. Therefore there is no sign of the 'Golden Period' in Klimt's landscape painting. In these paintings he came closer to the Neo-Impressionists or to the Pointillists. A tree, a lake, a meadow is made up of fine little brush-strokes. He did, however, use nuances of colour tones, rather than pure colour.

Just as he differentiated one style from another, so also he differentiated one subject from another. Nature does not enter into his portraits or into the cyclical pictures of birth, life and death, and, with the exception of one early painting, there are no living creatures in the landscapes. Nevertheless there are points of comparison in the composition of his portraits and landscape paintings, and it seems that in the summer he continued to work through the compositions which had occupied him during the winter in Vienna. The summer pictures provided enjoyment and enabled him to experiment without the constraints of patronage or contracts. It was a different matter with the portraits, one facet of his representation of woman.

Mäda Primavesi, 1912/13
Pencil, 56.1 × 36.8 cm

'Woman'

'Woman' occupies a central place in Klimt's work, isolated at times, at other times part of larger compositions. The picture of the interior of the old Burg Theatre had established his reputation as a painter of beautiful Viennese women, which soon resulted in private commissions for portraits. After 1896 he painted no more portraits of men on their own.

There are not as many portraits as his reputation might lead one to expect – only twenty-six in the total inventory of 222 paintings. The first of his less conventional portraits was the 'Portrait of Sonja Knips' of 1898, one of a series of portraits of wives or daughters of wealthy Viennese industrialists which culminated during the 'Golden Period' in the 1906 portrait of Fritza Riedler and the 1907 portrait of Adele Bloch-Bauer. In these the decorative female figure becomes one with the ornament.

Female figure standing turned
to the left, face towards the front
(Adele Bloch-Bauer), 1904/05
Black crayon, 55 × 34.8 cm

Head and limbs seem to be detached from the body; they float in a sea of gold and ornamentation, almost, it could be said, disturbing it. The identity of art and life, fulfilled at the highest level in the total work of art, is disturbed by the appearance of an individual's face. According to prevailing notions, a woman could more easily be absorbed into the picture than a man.

In 1909 a radical change in Klimt's style can be observed, in his portraits as in his other paintings. He stopped using gold in his paintings, the brush-stroke became wider, more restless. Klimt came close to Expressionism, without ever becoming an Expressionist painter. The cause of this change is still unknown. The figures became more tangible, there was less ornamentation. Shortly before his death Klimt returned to the conventional portraiture of his early years.

Klimt painted portraits in response to commissions, but he also contemplated the 'femme fatale'. Early allegorical works pointed the

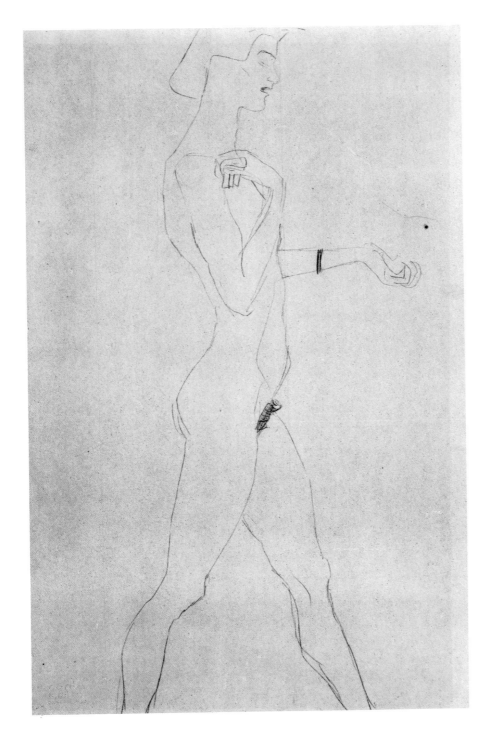

way towards powerfully symbolical representations of the feminine.
Woman appeared through metamorphosis as mermaid or water
serpent, as Danaë, Leda, Judith (figures drawn from classical antiquity
or from the bible).

The delicate and emotive subject of pregnancy gave rise to three of
Klimt's paintings. The most important example is 'Hope I', painted in
1903 for the Secession's exhibition of his work. The Minister of
Education, who was playing a key role in the dispute over the Faculty
pictures at the time, intervened and persuaded Klimt not to insist on
exhibiting the picture. It would probably have caused a scandal since it
showed a nude far advanced in pregnancy. She turns her head to look
out of the picture, and the poise of her figure and the expression on her
face represent both motherhood and lasciviousness. In the background the figures of a monster, illness and death, threaten the unborn
child. There is nothing but a narrow blue band behind the pregnant
woman to indicate the hope associated with the beginning of a new life.

Half-sketch of woman, left profile,
1906/07
Pencil, 55,2 × 34 cm

Theme and date suggest that the symbolic aspects of the painting may refer to the short life of Otto Zimmermann (22.6.1902–11.9.1902), the second son of Mizzi Zimmermann and Gustav Klimt. Although he never married the mothers of his children – he is known to have had three children, and fourteen women lodged paternity claims after his death – Klimt cared about them, as is shown by the correspondence with Mizzi Zimmermann which has recently come to light. The death of his son seems to have weighed so heavily upon him that he abandoned the tapestry pattern in the background and replaced it by the familiar motifs which had occurred first in the Faculty pictures, to be taken up again and again, for instance in the 'Procession of the Dead' (1903), the 'Three Ages of Woman' (1905), and 'Death and Life' (1911/16).

A further facet of Klimt's view of Woman can be observed in his drawings. More than 2000 drawings have survived, many of them female nudes. Apart from the female nude, shown from different viewpoints, Klimt drew lovers in various postures, women united in

Girl, front view, hands against her
cheek, 1910
Pencil, 55.9 × 36.2 cm

lesbian love, masturbating women, demonstrations of sexual organs,
pregnant women with and without an accompanying male figure. One
aspect of Woman is frequently in the foreground: her total availability.
Man – in this case Klimt – presents Woman as passive sexual object. Her
body is offered for Man's delectation as she lies quietly, often sleeping. It
is Man's fantasies that are aroused, even in the displays of lesbian love.

It is difficult to grasp Klimt's view of Woman in all its complexity. His
view was determined in part by close relationships with women – he
lived all his life with his mother and sisters – and it included elements of
motherhood with all its mysteries as well as the exploitability of Woman
as plaything and sexual object, and the besetting fear of seduction.
Independent Woman is represented only by Emilie Flöge, whose
portrait he painted in 1902. Her flowing 'reform dress' dissolves into
ornamentation, yet in spite of the stylised incorporeality there is an air of
radiant self-confidence emanating from the figure, just as Klimt
intended there to be.

Seated female figure, front view, 1908
Pencil, 56.5 × 37.2 cm

The Vienna Workshops and the Art Exhibition of 1908

After the 1905 departure of the artists of the new style from the Secession, the Vienna Workshops became the focal point of Jugendstil in the city. Josef Hoffmann and Koloman Moser did much to elevate the status of arts and crafts. They set up various workrooms (for a silversmith, for different types of metalwork, for bookbinding and leatherwork, for carpentry and lacquering, later also for fashion). They aimed to provide an alternative to cheap mass production, to produce quality goods for everyday use from simple materials which everyone could afford. They were concerned about healthy working conditions, and they opposed exploitation of the workers. These laudable intentions naturally increased prices; the notion that everyone could afford the products of the Vienna Workshops was an illusion. Nevertheless,

19

Trudl Flöge, 1916/17
Pencil, 55.9 × 36.8 cm

ideas originating in Vienna were influential all over Europe, and Jugendstil workshops sprang up everywhere. There were offshoots of the Vienna Workshops in Zürich, Berlin and New York. But their calculations were often hazy, and more and more capital had to be invested in their projects, with the result that by 1915 the fortune of the third co-founder, Fritz Waerndorfer, had been consumed in its entirety. He left the Workshops, which survived as a limited liability company until 1932, at which point they were forced into liquidation.

Although the Workshops foundered, their influence on arts and crafts should not be underestimated; it can still be discerned today. Our own sense of style and design has been formed in part by ideas current in the early years of the century.

Gustav Klimt had close links with the Workshops. It was probably owing to him that the Flöge Sisters' salon was fitted and furnished in the modern style by Hoffmann, and Klimt gave Emilie Flöge a number of presents made in the Workshops.

Woman's head, left profile, 1914
Pencil, 55.2 × 36.8 cm

In 1905 the Workshops won the greatest contract of all: they were commissioned to build and decorate a mansion in Brussels for the industrialist Adolphe Stoclet, and Klimt was one of the co-workers. It is the only house still preserved in its original form, and still inhabited, that was built and decorated by the Viennese group. It is only here that one can enter into the vision of life as a total work of art, as propagated by Gustav Klimt and his friends. They designed everything, so that uniformity of style could be ensured. Architecture, furniture, bathroom fittings, works of art, even the clothes which the Stoclets were to wear in their twenty rooms, were designed in Vienna.

Gustav Klimt drew actual-size working plans for the frieze which extends along both the fourteen-metre walls of the dining-room. They were done in tempera, water colours, gilt and silver bronze, chalks, pencil and opaque white, with precise instructions for the various craftsmen. The frieze consisted of fifteen sheets of white marble, inlaid with copper and silver plate, corals, semi-precious stones, gold mosaics, enamel and coloured fayence. The cost of the materials must have been approximately 100,000 crowns at the time, and Klimt's fee will have amounted to the same again. When one considers that a top civil servant earned some 7000 crowns a year, it is possible to have some idea of the vast expense of Palais Stoclet. Adolphe Stoclet never revealed the sum.

There is no 'action' in the frieze. Klimt's penchant for arts and crafts, and for pure ornamentation, is displayed more clearly than in the most decorative of his paintings. Trees, with flowers and birds, extend their branches over the whole length of both the walls, and on each wall there is a dancing girl, 'Expectation' on one side, 'Fulfilment', embraced in her lover's arms, on the other.

Klimt saw the frieze as the final stage of ornamental development; he refused to have the completed working plans, let alone the frieze itself, exhibited publicly in Vienna. He was not willing to expose his work to further vilification. At the Art Exhibition of 1908 the architect's plans and the designs for interior decoration of the Palais were shown, but not the frieze.

The Art Exhibition was organised by the artists of the new style who had left the Secession in 1905, in honour of the sixtieth anniversary of Emperor Franz Josef's accession to the throne. Klimt presided over the organising committee. The exhibition represented every branch of Austrian art. In 1909 a comparable show was organised, dedicated this time to work by artists from abroad. It was the last time that Klimt organised a public exhibition.

Josef Hoffmann was always responsible for the overall lay-out and design. He built a number of pavilions with a total of fifty-four rooms, set between terraces, courtyards and gardens. A coffee house and a

Half-figure, sleeping. c. 1915
Pencil 36.7 × 55.9 cm

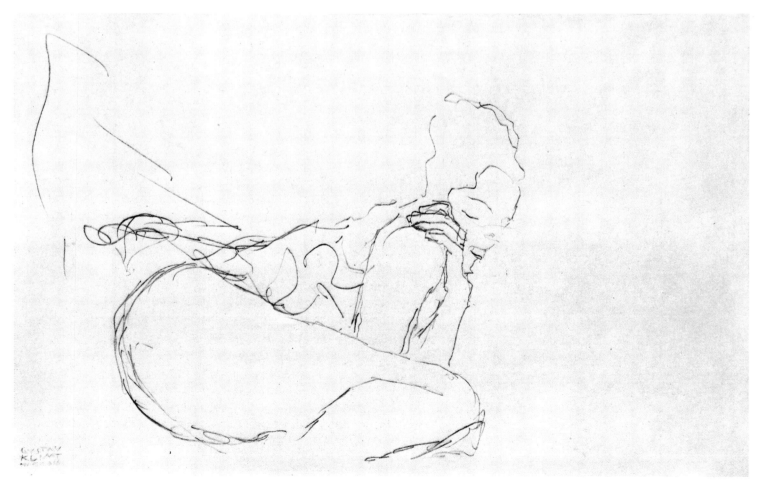

Recumbent half-figure, 1914/15
Pencil, 57.1 × 37.5 cm

summer theatre completed the facilities. The exhibition offered a comprehensive display of all the different branches of the art of style. There were paintings, architectural designs, sculpture, graphics, but also posters, graveyard art, ecclesiastical art, theatre art, arts and crafts, fashion and – the greatest innovation – artistic processes and products of children's play. There was also landscape art. The idea of the total work of art was in evidence again.

The central focus of the exhibition was Room 22, designed by Koloman Moser, in which sixteen paintings by Gustav Klimt were on display. In the adjoining room were some of his pencil drawings. Room 22, described by a contemporary as the 'Gustav Klimt cathedral of modern art', contained his well-known portraits, some landscape paintings, the 'Three Ages of Woman', 'Danae', the two versions of 'Water Serpents' and 'The Kiss'. 'The Kiss' is not only Klimt's most famous work, it has also become in some sort a symbol of Viennese Jugendstil, and it has to a certain extent been cheapened in the process.

Girl holding her arms above her head,
1905/06
Pencil, 44.5 × 30.5 cm

It has for instance been used as a poster, for advertising purposes or simply to put up on the wall. The picture, painted on gold ground reminiscent of Byzantine icons, before which the golden lovers embrace in a meadow of flowers, arouses hope and longing for harmony and happiness. Looked at more closely, particularly with its precursors in mind, it reveals other components too, which expose the dubiousness of this illusion. The precursors are 'Love' (1895), a pair of lovers in 'Philosophy', and the final scenes of the Beethoven Frieze and the Stoclet Frieze. At first glance 'The Kiss' seems to have little in common with these earlier pictures, but the underlying message is similar. The threat, that was symbolised by death, hostile forces or birds of prey, here takes the form of a precipice close by, over which the lovers might fall at any moment. The man remains the dominant figure, whose masculinity, expressed in 'The Kiss' by his strong, broad neck, reduces the woman to the passive rôle of sexual object.

Female figure, front view, arms raised,
1914
Pencil, 55.6 × 36.8 cm

A recently discovered sketch-book has a rapid sketch of lovers embracing, with the name 'Emilie' written in large letters beside it, and this seems to confirm what had long been suspected, namely that the picture is a self-portrait of Klimt with Emilie. Be that as it may, it would be wrong to lose sight of the more general relevance of the picture.

In the 1908 exhibition the picture was hung next to the 'Three Ages of Woman' – growth, maturity, decay – which has the same dimensions and is comparable in composition. Looked at together, they show the love that leads to procreation, human life in its different stages, and the threat of death that can strike at any moment, through perils (the precipice) or through old age. It is possible that Klimt conceived the pictures as forming a diptych, a unity.

In spite of all the different interpretations, comparisons and suggestions for sources, 'The Kiss' will remain Klimt's most popular and most intriguing picture. Its fascination is unchallenged.

Tribute and death

Klimt's development as an artist was unusual: success came early, to be followed by years of struggle. At the height of his early success he broke with tradition and set out on new paths. In his youth, he and his collaborators in the Company of Artists were honoured by the Emperor. He was just 26 when he received the Golden Order of Merit, and the Emperor's Prize followed two years later. But it was a long time before he received further honours from his native city. After he had left the Artists' House on the Ring, and become co-founder of the Vienna Secession, he won prizes and honours, but not in his own country. It was only in 1917 that he was made an honorary member of the Viennese Academy. The bitterness of his family led to the rejection of the tomb of honour which the City of Vienna offered to erect after his death.

Klimt lived his life within the family circle. His relative lack of

Woman in fur coat, 1916
Pencil, 50.2 × 32.5 cm

independence meant that he never left home to live elsewhere; he took care of his mother and two sisters financially. His lack of independence was noticeable also when he travelled.

It was a long time before Klimt left Vienna at all. Not until he had won the Emperor's Prize in 1890 did he cross the frontier into foreign parts. Up to that time he had scarcely travelled within the country, except to the places where the Company of Artists was commissioned to work on theatres. He spoke no foreign language, and he rapidly became homesick for Vienna. Nevertheless, two journeys contributed significantly to the development of his style. He first encountered Jugendstil art in Munich in 1890, and it quickly affected his painting. In 1903 he set off with a friend for Ravenna, where he studied the mosaics which had survived largely from the sixth century. He was so deeply impressed by these mosaics – the ornament, the figures, the gold ground – that covered the vaulted ceiling of the relatively small church that he returned there in the winter of the same year. These mosaics moved him to use gold more and more in his pictures, and were influential in the design of the Stoclet Frieze.

Further journeys to Florence and Upper Italy, to Berlin, Brussels, London, Munich and Prague, were usually prompted by his involvement in exhibitions in these places. In 1909 he travelled to Paris and to Spain with Carl Moll, but even this extended journey did not increase his enthusiasm for foreign travel. When he did leave Vienna, he liked most of all to spend his time in the familiar surroundings of the Attersee.

It was in Vienna that he felt at home. His daily routine was entirely regular. He rose early and took a long walk to the café where he breakfasted. His friends knew that they could find him there. Then he walked all the way to his studio, where he worked all day without a break. In the evening he often went to the theatre, or he met up with friends in coffee-houses or bars. He was very concerned about his health, and Emilie had to be told about the slightest catarrh. Whenever she was away from Vienna, he commented on the weather in his daily letters.

There is general agreement that Klimt was not a talkative man, that he relaxed only in the company of his closest friends, but also that he had a certain wit, which is evident at times in his paintings and drawings.

Klimt suffered a stroke on 11 January 1918, from which he did not recover. He died on 6 February, and was buried four days later in the cemetery in Hietzing. His death mask shows a completely unfamiliar face, since his beard had been shaved during the last days of his life.

Klimt left no self-portrait. He did not keep a diary, and wrote few letters. But there is one undated type-written text which is preserved in the City Library in Vienna:

„Commentary on a non-existent self-portrait:

I can paint and I can draw. I believe that, and a few others say that they

Recumbent figure turned to the right, 1913
Red and blue pencil, 36.8 × 57.2 cm

28

Woman's head with closed eyes, 1915/16
Pencil, 55.9 × 36.5 cm

believe it too. Yet I am not entirely sure that it is true. I am sure of two things only:

1. There is no self-portrait of me. I am not interested in myself as 'material for a picture', rather in other people, especially women, but even more, in other phenomena. I am convinced that as a person I am not particularly interesting. There's nothing remarkable to be seen in me. I am a painter, one who paints every day from morning till evening. Figures, landscapes, occasionally portraits.

2. Words, spoken or written, do not come easily to me, especially not when I'm supposed to be saying something about myself or my work. If I have to write a simple letter I get just as scared as if I was going to be sea-sick. So people will have to do without an artistic or literary self-portrait. Which is just as well. Anyone who wants to find out about me – as artist, that's all that's of interest – should look at my pictures attentively and look to discover from them what I am, and what I want."

Biographical Table

1862   Gustav Klimt born 14 July in Baumgarten (today XIVth District of Vienna), second of seven children of the gold-engraver Ernst Klimt from Bohemia and Anna née Finster of Vienna.

1876   Klimt leaves school with 'very good' certificate. Obtains 2-year scholarship to study at new School of Arts and Crafts attached to Austrian Museum of Art and Industry, under Rieser, Minnigerode and Hrachowina. Brother Ernst Klimt joins him there in 1877. Klimt brothers and Franz Matsch transfer to Ferdinand Laufberger's painting class in 1878.

1879   Klimt brothers and Franz Matsch commissioned by Laufberger to execute sgraffiti in Vienna's Art History Museum.They take part in preparations for Makart's pageant in honour of the Emperor's Silver Wedding Jubilee.

1880   Klimt brothers and Matsch paint 4 ceiling pictures for Palais Sturany in Vienna and receive first commission from theatre architects Fellner and Helmer, for ceiling picture for Spa Rooms in Karlsbad.

1881   Death of Laufberger. Further studies with Julius Victor Berger. Klimt brothers and Matsch set up joint 'Company of Artists' and are commissioned to contribute to 'Allegory and Emblem'.

1883   After completion of studies, Company moves to own studio. Klimt works for 'Allegory and Emblem'.

1886   Klimt paints 2 ceiling pictures in Karlsbad theatre, paints curtains jointly with Ernst Klimt and Matsch. Work begins on ceiling and lunette paintings for the 2 stairways in the new Burg Theatre.

1888   Emperor's highest award, Golden Order of Merit, granted to Company for work on Burg Theatre. Klimt paints 'Auditorium in Old Burg Theatre'.

1890   Klimt receives Emperor's Prize with 400 guilders for Burg Theatre painting. Company begins work on 40 spandrel and intercolumnar paintings for stairway of Vienna Art History Museum.

1891   Membership of Vienna Association of Visual Artists.

1896   Klimt commissioned to paint 3 faculty pictures for university hall ceiling – 'Philosophy', 'Medicine' and 'Jurisprudence' – and 10 spandrel pictures on related themes. Matsch takes over other pictures.

1897   Klimt and some 20 other artists leave the Association of Visual Artists and found the Secession, with Klimt as president. First landscapes.

1898   Klimt designs poster for Secession's first exhibition. Preliminary compositions for faculty pictures criticized and only conditionally accepted.

1900   Unfinished faculty picture 'Philosophy' shown at VIIth Secession exhibition. Petition of 87 professors against its being positioned on university hall ceiling. With this picture Klimt wins the gold medal for foreign artists at autumn exhibition in Paris.

1901   'Medicine' exhibited at Xth Secession exhibition. Violent protest in press and parliament.

1902   'Beethoven Frieze' exhibited at XIVth Secession exhibition built round Max Klinger's Beethoven statue. Klimt's frieze still exists, all other murals were destroyed after the exhibition.

1903   Klimt impressed by visit to Ravenna. Josef Hoffmann and Koloman Moser found Vienna Workshops, much influenced by Klimt. 80 of Klimt's works exhibited by the Secession, including the three faculty pictures. Art commission considers hanging faculty pictures in Modern Gallery.

1905   Klimt terminates contract for faculty pictures and repays advance in full. Klimt and friends leave the Secession.

1906   Travels to Brussels and London in connection with Stoclet Frieze. First square portrait of 'golden period'.

1907   Faculty pictures finally completed, exhibited in final form. Height of 'golden period'.

1908   Klimt organizes exhibition of so-called 'Klimt Group', the 'Artists of Style' who had left the Secession. 'The Kiss,' one of 16 Klimt pictures exhibited, is bought by Austrian State Gallery.

1909   End of 'golden period'. Klimt organises exhibition for last time. Travels in autumn to Paris and Spain.

1910   Participates in Venice Biennale.

1911   Participates in international exhibition in Rome, awarded 1st prize for 'Death and Life'. Moves into new studio; Company's original studio due to be demolished.

1917   Honorary membership of Academy of Fine Arts in Vienna and Munich.

1918   Klimt suffers a stroke on 11 January and dies on 6 February leaving numerous paintings unfinished.

The Colour Plates

46

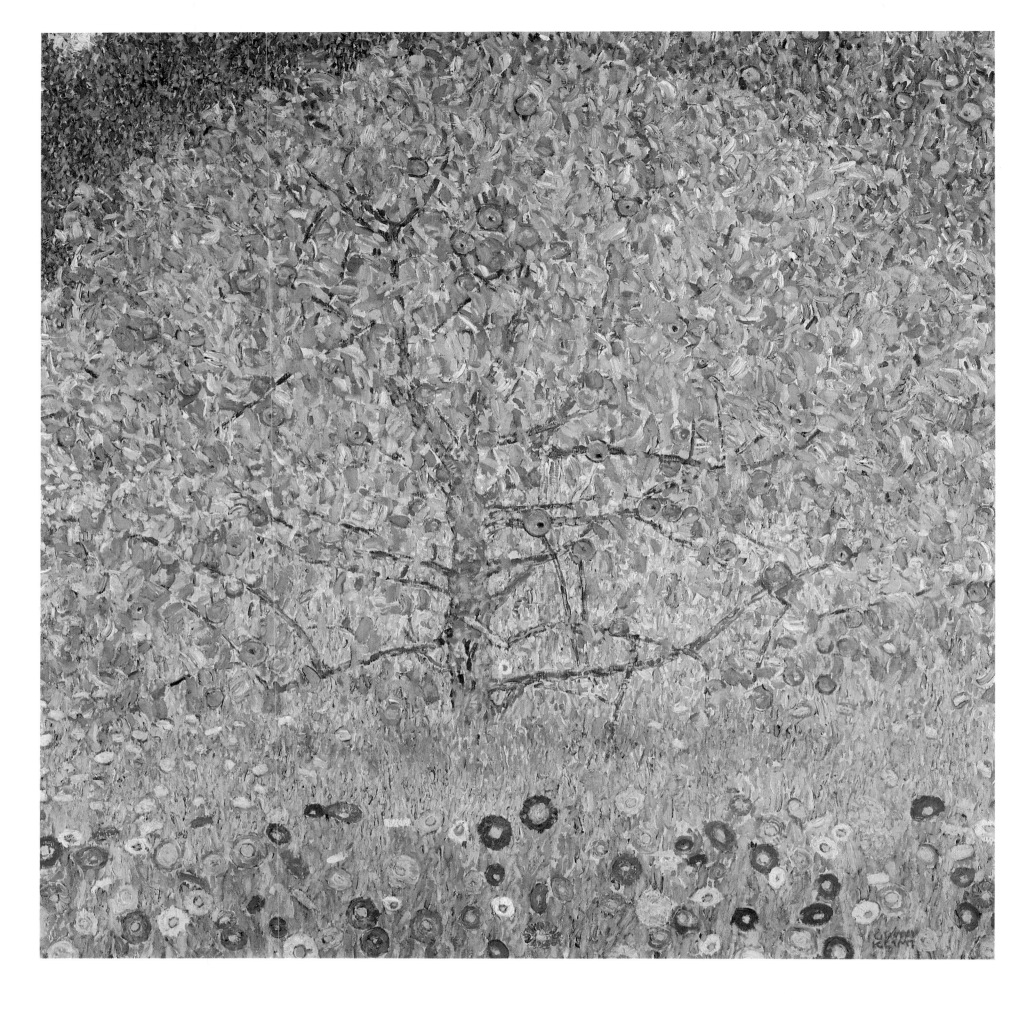

60

64